Craig-y-Nos...

Adelina Patti's

Gwyn Briwnant Jones

Gomer

First Impression – 2004

ISBN 1 84323 358 4

© Gwyn Briwnant Jones

Gwyn Briwnant Jones has asserted his right under the
Copyright, Designs and Patents Act, 1988,
to be identified as Author of this Work.

All rights reserved. No part of this book may be
reproduced, stored in a retrieval system, or transmitted
in any form or by any means, electronic, electrostatic, magnetic tape,
mechanical, photocopying, recording or otherwise without permission in
writing from the publishers, Pont Books, Gomer Press, Llandysul,
Ceredigion.

*Printed in Wales at
Gomer Press, Llandysul, Ceredigion SA44 4JL*

Adelina Patti (1843-1919) was the most famous and wealthy opera singer of her day. She was a mega-star before the term was ever invented by media tycoons a century or so later. Even now, 85 years since her passing, it is no exaggeration to regard her, still, as a phenomenon. The operatic world lay at her feet; she was feted wherever she went and was treated like royalty.

Patti could have lived anywhere in the world but chose to live in Wales at Craig-y-nos, where she created a luxurious haven, equipped with every device of the age, where she was attended – and worshipped – by a retinue of servants for over forty years. Excepting the times when she was on tour, Patti was destined to spend the greater part of her life in the remote and romantic location at the head of the Tawe valley, north of Swansea.

Physically diminutive (being only 5ft-2ins in height, possessing a 17 inch waist and fitting her feet into size 2 shoes) the dark-eyed Patti held a fascination, particularly for men, throughout her life. Her list of intimate friends included the Prince of Wales (later, King Edward VII); composers Rossini and Verdi; financier Alfred de Rothschild; actor and impresario Henry Irving; Baron de Reuter, founder of the news agency – together with many other prominent personalities of the day.

Dame Nellie Melba later declared that Patti possessed 'perhaps the most golden voice [she had] ever heard, its timbre exquisite, her diction pellucid' and on another occasion, in 1888, early in her own career she stated, 'I am going to Paris . . . whatever happens. I do not care if I never sing again. To hear Patti and Jean de Reszke would make up for anything, any sacrifice.'[1]

In addition to purely vocal skills, Patti apparently conveyed an impression of singing to each member of a vast audience in a very personal, almost individual, way. Moreover, whilst lacking the greatest volume, she could nonetheless project her brilliant, agile voice to the furthest reaches of a grand auditorium, even in competition with orchestra and chorus.

Born of Italian parents in Madrid in 1843, but brought up in America, Patti's rare talent had emerged at an early age – she gave her first concert in 1851 at New York's Tripler Hall, when she was eight years of age. She was only sixteen when she performed in her first opera, *Lucia di Lammermoor*, at the New York Academy of Music. As she emerged on the stage that evening of 24 November, 1859, she was greeted initially by a silence which, only gradually, it seemed, gave way to polite, luke-warm applause. Without the benefit of advance publicity, the audience must have been surprised – stunned even – to see this child-like figure about to assume the demanding role of the *protagonista*. But, by the end of that performance, Patti had created a positive furore, which was demonstrated 'with recalls, bouquets, wreaths etc., etc.' according to the *New York Herald*. She became a celebrity overnight, displaying vocal skill of a quality far beyond her years and experience. Another contemporary critic wrote in the *New York Tribune*, 'Her voice is clear and excellent; the brilliant execution she begins with at the

The Royal Opera House, Covent Garden *c.* 1865.

(GBJ Collection)

outset of her career – she is only turned sweet sixteen – ranks with that where the best singers end.'

Thus began one of the most remarkable stage careers of all time. By 1861, when Patti was just 18, she had appeared in six leading roles at the Royal Opera Covent Garden, a venue to which she returned each spring for twenty-five consecutive years. She was at her zenith during this quarter century, when she pursued her career mainly in Europe. The routine generally adopted during this period commenced with the Covent Garden season, followed by an autumn concert tour in the UK and, after Christmas, visits to the French Riviera and engagements in the principal opera houses of Europe. The following spring, the cycle continued. Patti's usual practice was to rent a villa in each of the main capitals in turn; when in London, she stayed at Pierrepoint House, Clapham Park, which she re-named Rossini Villa. Her career – and in consequence, the vast fortune she accumulated – were based on her willingness to travel; for over forty years she devoted herself to the incessant round of touring and performing, both in opera houses and concert halls, around the world. Her success owed as much to hard work and dedication as to her prodigious talent.

She sang before all the crowned heads of Europe and amongst many prestigious engagements over the years were regular appearances before Queen Victoria at Buckingham Palace and Windsor, originally it is thought, at the behest of the Prince of Wales – always one of her most fervent admirers. They first met at her concert in Montreal on 24 August 1860, when Patti was seventeen years of age and the Prince a year older.

Notable characteristics which accompanied Patti throughout her life were her love of costume, role-playing and socialising, and during her early years particularly, Paris – with its vibrant social life –

held a special appeal for her. There, when in her early twenties, Patti was introduced to the Marquis de Caux, an equerry of Napoleon III; De Caux was Patti's senior by eighteen years. An excellent horseman and brilliant conversationalist, he possessed all the requisite social skills and graces to introduce Patti to court circles, a factor which she quickly appreciated. They were married in London, on 27 July 1868, at the Roman Catholic Church in Clapham. In retrospect, it appears the union was mainly a matter of convenience; that it was not successful became quickly apparent. One particular bone of contention was De Caux's attempt to get his wife to relinquish her stage career but the impecunious Marquis eventually agreed with reluctance that she should continue (for what he then thought would be a maximum of five years). Unfortunately for De Caux, one Ernesto Nicolini – a French tenor with an Italianate name – and a noted libertine and philanderer, was one of Patti's colleagues at this time. Initially Patti took an instant and acute dislike to him, but Nicolini persisted and within a comparatively short period her response changed dramatically and she embarked on an extended period of notoriety: the scandal swept Europe. Her marriage to De Caux was ostensibly over – they separated in 1877 – although the divorce was not absolute until July, 1885.

Patti's professional status seemed unaffected; indeed, her career advanced from strength to strength. During a most successful tour of Italy in 1877 she made her debut as Violetta in *La Traviata* at La Scala, Milan and when she appeared in Genoa in December, Verdi wrote '. . . Patti . . . was received with indescribable enthusiasm. She deserves it, for she is an artist by nature, so perfect that perhaps there has never been her equal . . . a marvellous voice, a very pure style of singing, a stupendous artist with a charm and naturalness which no one else has.'[2]

As Patti and Nicolini toured the opera houses of Europe together, the high moral tone of the period generated severe criticism – even ostracization by sections of society. It was a factor which could have influenced Patti's decision to seek relief from the searching and critical gaze of the world. Furthermore, the exhausting routine of travel and performance must have contributed to this decision and, predictably, Patti yearned to establish a home of her own. When consideration was duly given to the matter of location, she was fortunate that she had the whole world from which to choose.

Somewhat surprisingly, perhaps, Patti was no stranger to Wales. Even before she had seen Craig-y-nos, Patti and Nicolini had stayed at Waterton Hall, near Bridgend and also with Sir Henry Hussey Vivian, M.P., at Cadoxton Lodge, Neath. Sir Henry, aware of Patti's search for a country retreat, is the person accredited with drawing Craig-y-nos to her attention.

There seems little doubt that when the diva first saw the house nestling amidst the attractive, rugged terrain at the head of the Tawe valley, she immediately fell in love with it. Possibly, the romantic location reminded her of her debut role as Lucia in Donizetti's opera or, perhaps the wild, remote situation possessed a degree of isolation which especially appealed to her but, for whatever reason, Craig-y-nos proved to be Patti's own particular 'Home Sweet Home' for the remainder of her life.

The enormous popularity of the ballad of that name may be attributed to the great wave of Victorian confidence which then manifested itself in travel, exploration and commerce. Under such circumstances, it was easy, and natural, to sentimentalise over memories of times and places relinquished in the quest for wordly success and fortune; the words and music of the song tugged effortlessly and relentlessly at the heart-strings of those far from home.

The house and location which appealed so strongly to Patti in 1875.

(The Brecon Museum)

Written by Sir Henry Bishop in what purported to be the form of a Sicilian melody, 'Home Sweet Home' was quickly established by Patti as her signature tune; she sang it at virtually all her performances, even interpolating it into the established operatic repertoire, often in the guise of a 'lesson song'. It followed her wherever she went; no audience, seemingly, would release her until it had been sung.

Few could rival the diva's interpretation and many listeners found it difficult to keep a dry eye during her performance, yet no one seemed in the least concerned at the incongruity of the words as Patti sang . . .

An exile from home, splendour dazzles in vain,
O give me my lowly thatched cottage again . . .

By the time Patti was rumoured to have spent approximately £100,000 on extensions and renovations (*c.* £100 million by today's values?) there was certainly nothing lowly or humble about Craig-y-nos Castle, but the chief sentiments of the song remained as meaningful to Adelina as any of her listeners.

To claim that she fell in love with the house, which she always referred to as a Castle, is no exaggeration. During a tour of America in 1885, when outlining her forthcoming itinerary to a *New York Herald* reporter, Patti added . . .

> 'Then I shall return to dear Craig-y-nos in Wales. It is such a beautiful place with splendid scenery . . . I think Wales is one of the most beautiful spots in the world. It is so quiet, so resting (sic) and yet the scenery [is] so full of grandeur.

Then, a year or so later, she stated . . .

> 'All the time I don't spend at Craig-y-nos seems to me time lost. I should not give a snap of my finger for my brilliant career had it not procured for me a delicious country retreat and the kind of anchorage that exactly suits me'.[3]

The site of the house was originally referred to in early documents as Bryn Melin but the house itself, designed by architect T. H. Wyatt and built between 1841 and 1843 for a local client, Rice Davies Powell, was known as Craig-y-nos. When Powell was forced to sell some years later, another local owner held possession briefly before

Adelina saw the house in 1875. Although she was immediately enchanted, particularly with the location, she had to wait until 1878 before the sale was completed, for £3500. With Nicolini's encouragement and collaboration she made major alterations, introducing electricity, improving the heating and adding an ice-making plant, a clock tower, an aviary, a conservatory and a winter garden. Further land was purchased as the estate itself was enlarged and landscaped, with terraced lawns, a variety of gardens and an ornamental lake. Nicolini thoroughly relished his new role as a member of the landed gentry and derived great pleasure from the country pursuits of shooting and fishing. But of all the various improvements the most significant, undoubtedly, was and is Patti's private theatre. This jewel happily survives today in near original condition – a factor which would surely please the diva – although nowadays it rarely hosts world-famous singers worthy of such a fine and historic location.

Throughout the period of her greatest popularity and wealth, Patti entertained lavishly at the Castle. In 1891, for example, on the occasion of the inauguration of the theatre, important guests travelled in special railway carriages, via the nearby Penwyllt railway station, coming and going over a period of several weeks. Prince Henry of Battenburg was one who travelled by special train from Swansea – where he was staying at Clyne Castle – for a Gala performance in his honour. Patti's hospitality on that occasion was lavish. Signor Arditi, the orchestral conductor, composer and lifelong friend, estimated that 450 bottles of champagne were consumed during the celebrations.

Over the years, Patti was the recipient of countless expensive gifts from her many admirers, including Queen Victoria, other royalty and heads of state. She, in turn, was generous to those around her

A close-up view of Craig-y-nos before modification and enlargement by Patti and Nicolini.

(The Brecon Museum)

and took particular pleasure in entertaining Welsh singers at the Castle. A 1904 account, '*A command to appear before Madame Patti*' relates how a special railway saloon was placed at the disposal of Mr Moss Joseph to travel from Swansea. When he arrived at Penwyllt he was met by the coachman and driven to the Castle in a carriage and pair, along the stretch of roadway especially constructed at Patti's expense to improve access between Castle and station. On arrival at the Castle, Mr Moss Joseph's welcome was complete when he was granted a room for the night.

Both Castle and estate contributed significantly to the local economy. In its hey-day, during the Patti-Nicolini years, around forty indoor staff were employed there, with an almost equal number

Patti's immaculate house and estate shortly after the opening of the theatre (left side). Part of what later became known as the Patti Pavilion, in Swansea, is visible on the extreme right.

(The National Library of Wales)

in the gardens and estate, although this declined dramatically after Patti's retirement. Such employment was invaluable in an area with few alternatives to farming or coal-mining. Local produce was obtained for use in the Castle whenever possible and Patti's generous contributions to the deprived and elderly of the area were legion. Special charity concerts were given specifically to raise funds for this purpose.

Indeed, these concerts, together with performances in her own theatre at Craig-y-nos, served to ease Patti toward retirement. Wales saw both the inaugural and the final charity concerts; the first occasion was a joint event with Nicolini in Swansea, in 1882; the last was also in Swansea, in September 1907. Between these occasions Patti organised additional charity concerts at Pontardawe, Brecon, Neath and Cardiff. She also appeared at the National Eisteddfod of Wales at Caernarfon, on 15 September 1886 (when she sang '*Caro mio ben*' and took part in *Elijah,* with Eos Morlais Thomas) and, later, in 1889, when the Eisteddfod was in Brecon she enchanted a huge audience estimated at approximately 12,000 by singing 'Hen

A more recent view of Crig-y-nos (2000) set against the majestic backcloth provided by the Brecon Beacons.

(Knight Frank, Hereford)

The Patti Theatre in 2000, revealing the quality of the original workmanship and the care with which this has been preserved down the years.

(Knight Frank, Hereford)

Wlad fy Nhadau', the National Anthem, in Welsh. It is little wonder that Patti was held in such high esteem, for in addition to being a 'Queen of Song', her generosity – particularly in Brecon and the Tawe valley – earned for her the additional title of 'Queen of Hearts'.

With Patti's divorce from De Caux becoming absolute on 15 July 1885, preparations were quickly made for her marriage to Nicolini. A civil cermony was arranged at Swansea on 9 June 1886 and the following day a church service was held at Ystradgynlais Parish Church. This was the time when Patti briefly considered purchasing a house in north Wales from J. E. Greaves, the quarry owner; this was Dolfriog, at Nantmor near Aberglaslyn. Having lived 'in sin' at Craig-y-nos for seven years, the idea of an additional property at this time might have been symbolic of the new union but there is no suggestion of a permanent move from Craig-y-nos and the idea fell through.

ALBERT HALL, SWANSEA.

Programme

OF A

GRAND MORNING CONCERT

ARRANGED BY

MADAME ADELINA

PATTI=NICOLINI

Assisted by the following Eminent Artistes (who kindly give their valuable services):

(By permission of Messrs. Stedle Bros., Photographers, Swansea).

MISS MARIANNE EISSLER,
(SOLO VIOLIN),

MISS CLARA EISSLER,
(SOLO HARP),

MADAME HANNAH JONES,

MR. DURWARD LELY,   **MR. NORMAN SALMOND,**

SIGNOR BONETTI,   **SIGNOR A. ROMILI,**
(SOLO PIANOFORTE,)

CONDUCTOR = = = = Mr. WILHELM GANZ,

TO BE GIVEN

On THURSDAY, JULY 12th, 1894,

AT 2.30 P.M.,

FOR THE BENEFIT OF THE SWANSEA HOSPITAL AND POOR OF THE NEIGHBOURHOOD OF CRAIG-Y-NOS CASTLE.

HUDSON & KEARNS, Printers, London, S.E.

Patti's portraits still adorned the Music Room in 2000.

(Knight Frank, Hereford)

Patti and Nicolini were to enjoy a further twelve years together, although Nicolini's health declined gradually, making the final years increasingly difficult. He suffered from disorders of the liver and kidneys and, in the belief that sea air would be of benefit, he moved to Langland Bay to convalesce. Patti, who disliked the bracing seaside atmosphere, chose to remain at Craig-y-nos, but travelled by train to and from Swansea each day – a considerable inconvenience. Nicolini later sought further benefit at Brighton and on the Riviera, but all to no avail; he died at Pau, in January 1898. With his demise there ended finally the joyous days of extravagant entertainment at the Castle, when Craig-y-nos had been alive with guests, parties and music.

Barely over a year later, Patti re-married. The wedding took place at St. Michael's Roman Catholic Church, Brecon, on 25 January 1899; the groom was Baron Rolf Cederstrom, a Swedish nobleman.

Nowadays, the good-looking Cederstrom would be regarded as something of a 'toy-boy' – he was Patti's junior by some nineteen years, being 37 to Patti's 56.

If Patti and Nicolini had enjoyed the fruits of their collective earnings with endless rounds of entertaining, midst all the luxuries and elegance of the age, Cederstrom saw things differently. He had entered Patti's life after her retirement from the operatic stage and although she still appeared in concerts, she no longer commanded the enormous fees of earlier days with the same frequency. Even with the benefit of shrewd investment of the not inconsiderable Patti fortune – under the guidance of financier Alfred de Rothschild – Cederstrom saw that the former life-style would be difficult to maintain on the reduced income. The days of lavish entertainment dwindled as the great diva's career drew to a close and as Cederstrom exercised tight control of financial matters. Furthermore, the Baron was hardly enchanted at the prospect of living in Nicolini's shadow at Craig-y-nos. Within two years, he persuaded Patti to sell the Castle, ostensibly so they might spend more time with his family in Sweden. Craig-y-nos was subsequently placed on the market during the spring of 1901 but failed to attract adequate offers and Patti, from all accounts, was happy to withdraw the sale that summer. She remained at 'dear Craig-y-nos' to the end of her days.

Perhaps the most important development during the twilight of Patti's career was her agreement with 'The Gramophone Company' to record her voice. Sound recording, then in its infancy, was largely experimental, with some of the pioneering techniques yielding indifferent results. Nor were the commercial advantages fully appreciated until 1902, when Fred Gaisberg of 'The Gramophone Company' (which later became HMV) recorded the voice of a

Patti's guests who arrived by train encountered this first glimpse of the Castle on their journey from the station; the view has changed little over the years and may still be enjoyed today.

(Knight Frank, Hereford)

virtually unknown Enrico Caruso – against the specific wishes of his superiors. The artistic and commercial success of that venture, however, was instantaneous and the importance of the gramophone became firmly established, virtually overnight.

Patti had previously been approached to record but had steadfastly refused to co-operate until, possibly, she may have been influenced by the sweeping success of the Caruso recordings. She eventually agreed to a test recording, with the proviso that if the results were displeasing, the master disc would be destroyed. Such was Patti's status and influence in the world of opera that, even though over sixty years of age, she was able to dictate her own terms. Her unwillingness to travel to a recording studio, for example, meant that the recording equipment and engineers had to be transported to Craig-y-nos. Thus the brothers Will and Fred Gaisberg travelled by rail to Penwyllt, in 1905. But even after they had set up their equipment in the Castle, in two large bedrooms which had been cleared and placed at their disposal, they were delayed a few days while Patti allowed herself further time to become acclimatized and fully comfortable with the idea. While they were kept waiting, Adelina ordered her staff: 'Those two nice gentlemen – let them have champagne for dinner tonight to make up for their disappointment'. The brothers Gaisberg, together with Landon Ronald the accompanist, remained at Craig-y-nos for a week. Patti, through her solicitor, had negotiated a fee of £1000 for her contribution.[4]

The gramophone on which Patti eventually played her own records and which, most probably, was presented to her by the gramophone company, was purchased by Mr Tom Powell of Ystradgynlais at the time of the Sale of the Castle's contents in 1920. Many will argue that examples such as this 1904 'state of the art'

Adelina Patti's 1904 'state of the art' gramophone. Although documentary evidence is lacking, this would almost certainly have been a gift from the Gramophone Company. *(National Museums & Galleries of Wales, St Fagans)*

instrument provide the most faithful reproduction of acoustic recordings of the period. It was later presented by Mr Powell's family to the National Museum of Wales, and is now in the collections of the Museums and Galleries of Wales, Museum of Welsh Life, St. Fagans.

Whilst the recordings of 1905 leave much to be desired when compared with more modern results, we are fortunate that they pleased Patti sufficiently to ensure their survival and eventual publication. Nowadays, they are regarded by modern listeners more used to digital, multi-channel recordings, as little more than scratchy curiosities from a past age. But we should not be swayed by the deficiencies and limitations of the recording process but concentrate upon positive aspects of Patti's performance and technique. There are those who regret that even the primitive 1905 technology had not been available many years earlier, to leave us with a much better impression of Patti's true stature, when she was at the height of her fame. Nonetheless, even though we are grateful for the survival of the Patti recordings, we must recognise that they are, at best, but impressions of a singer past her prime.

As with so many performers who spend a lifetime before the public, Patti found it difficult to relinquish the attention and adulation which had accompanied her all her life. Her last professional operatic engagement was at Nice, in 1897, but her concert career continued with tours in the UK, Europe and north America. During the twilight of her career a succession of so-called 'Farewell' performances were arranged, particularly in the United States, a factor which may have contributed to some indifference at the time of her last U.S. tour in 1903/4; this failed to enjoy the success of previous visits. Patti's audiences in Europe, however, appeared more faithful and concert tours throughout Britain and the continent continued until her final professional appearance at the Royal Albert Hall in 1911.

Even this was not the last occasion for Patti to sing in public, for she appeared one more time at the Albert Hall when she contributed to a War Benefit Concert, on 24 October 1914. On this poignant

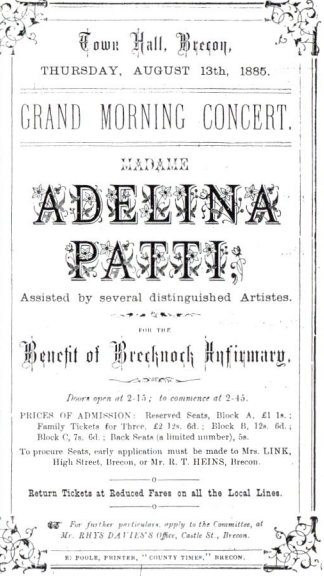

(Brecon Museum and the City and County of Cardiff Library)

occasion she sang Mozart's '*Voi che sapete*' and, inevitably, 'Home Sweet Home'.

As the twentieth century progressed, Craig-y-nos gradually became a quieter, more sombre place, although Patti still sang to please herself and could be heard from the roadway outside the walls, as she walked the gardens.

(The British Library, London)

Solo Piano	...	...	...	...	"Staccato Etude"	...	...	...	...	*Rubinstein.*

MISS MATHILDE VERNE.

Vocal Waltz	...	...	...	...	... "Il Bacio" ...	...	...	...	...	*Arditi.*

MADAME ADELINA PATTI.

(The Baroness Rolf Cederström.)

SULLE, sulle, labbra, se potessi dolce un bacio ti darei
Tutte ti direi le dolcezze dell'amor
Sempre, assisa te d'appresso, mille gaudii ti direi
Ed i palpiti udirei che rispondono al mio cor;
Gemme e perle non desio
Non son vaga d'altro affetto,
Un tuo sguardo è il mio diletto
Un tuo bacio è il mio tesor
Vieni ah! vien più non tardare
Vieni ah vieni a me d'appresso.
Ah! vein nell'ebbrezza d'un amplesso
Ch'io viva, ch'io viva sol d'amor;
Sulle labbra se potessi, dolce un bacio ti darei
Ah! vien d'appresso a me,
Ah! si vien d'appresso a me.

English Version.

BRIGHTLY dawns upon me morning's gladsome ray,
Returning, yes, returning from my exile far away.
Ah! how slowly wing'd the hours, when pining on a foreign strand,
And far remote from thee, my native land.

Fancy fly, fancy fly swiftly, o'er the raging main;
To my ear, to my eye, paint the home of youth again.
Dream, oh thou fond heart, of the merry days of old;
Think, oh thou lone heart, friends have not grown cold.

Evening comes thro' my dream, the vesper chimes are ringing;
I see the tapers gleam, and hear the maidens singing;
Hallowed and happy spot, thou knoweth nought of sadness,
Will it be, then, my lot to share again thy gladness?

Ah! yes, ah! yes, again in my home,
I'll ne'er from the loved scenes of fatherland roam!
Ah! joy now thrills my throbbing heart,
From thee, dear home, I'll ne'er depart!

Luigi Arditti, the composer, is largely forgotten today, but for this one song 'Il Bacio', which also reflects Patti's sentimental attitude towards her home – particularly as she was way from it for such extended periods.

Over the years, some deterioration was naturally noticed in her voice, but there was still magic in her performances. Sir Henry J. Wood, who accompanied her during the 1914 engagement recalled, 'We rehearsed "Voi che sapete". I felt the marvellous even-ness of her warm quality. Her voice was not powerful but it excelled anything I had imagined in red-rose-like quality and voluptuous sweetness . . . It was truly wonderful and I was entranced.' Even His Majesty, King George V

was moved to note in his diary, 'Patti sang, wonderfully still'.[5]

Patti's illustrious career had taken her to the leading opera houses of Europe and the Americas and she had performed in the major concert halls of the world. It continued virtually without pause from the time of her operatic debut in 1859, until her last operatic performance in Nice in 1897. Even the final decade, before the last professional appearance in 1911, had been punctuated by strenuous concert tours in Britain and America.

Adelina Patti died at Craig-y-nos on 27 September 1919; she lay at rest in her private chapel at the Castle and at the Roman Catholic

Chapel, Kensal Green, for eight months, until her remains were eventually buried at Peré Lachaise Cemetery, in Paris, on 29 May 1920. But those able to visit the Castle in the enchanting reaches of the upper Tawe valley, particularly the Craig-y-nos Theatre and less obviously perhaps, the remains of the little station at Penwyllt – Patti's gateway to the world – will appreciate that some of her magic endures . . . still.

The station at Penwyllt, which changed its name in 1903 to Craig-y-nos. Adelina Patti's private stone-built waiting-room is on the right.

Acknowledgements

The author is much indebted to the work of Dr John F. CONE, published as *Adelina Patti: Queen of Hearts* (1994) Scolar Press, Aldershot. Readers who seek further information are directed to this detailed and well-researched account.

Additional information was drawn from published material by David Brinn, David S. Downey, Ivor Wynne Jones, Ethel Rosate-Lunn and W. S. K. Thomas.

Staff at the following institutions have also been most helpful and extended the writer's knowledge by producing material, which, most pleasantly, was occasionally of a primary nature: The Brecon Museum; The British Library, London; The City and County of Cardiff Library; The National Library of Wales, Aberystwyth; The National Museums & Galleries of Wales; The National Railway Museum, York; The Royal Commission on Ancient and Historical Monuments in Wales.

Private individuals who have also been supportive are: Dr Stuart Owen-Jones, Cardiff; Dr and Mrs Penny Jones, owners of Craig-y-nos 1994/5–2000; Sue Drew, the present owner's secretary/representative; Mrs Jean Ewart Jones, Cardiff; Mr D. G. Rees, Cambourne.

Illustrations are acknowledged appropriately but the portraits of Patti at Brecon Museum and the colour images of Craig-y-nos produced by Knight Frank of Hereford for the 2000 Sale Brochure have been particularly appreciated, as have the superb colour prints of the Patti gramophone, organised by Meinwen Ruddock and taken especially for this publication by the photographic unit at the National Museums and Galleries of Wales, St. Fagans.

Scources of specific quotations are as follows:

[1] see *Adelina Patti; Queen of Hearts*, J.F. CONE (1994) p. 180/1.
[2] in CONE (1994) p. 129.
[3] in CONE (1994) p. 134.
[4] see *Music on Record*, F.W. GAISBERG (1947) p. 86/8.
[5] in CONE (1994) p. 8.